# Sock and Glove

Creating Charming Softy Friends

from Cast-off Socks and Gloves

Miyako Kanamori

HOME

**Miyako Kanamori** was born in Japan in 1970. She has worked on planning and design for a stuffed animal manufacturer and also designed original products for Southern Accents, a household goods store in Chigasaki, Japan. She is the author of *DOG? or ZOO?*

**A HOME BOOK**
**Published by the Penguin Group**
**Penguin Group (USA) Inc.**
**375 Hudson Street, New York, New York 10014, USA**
Penguin Group (Canada), 90 Eglinton Avenue East, Suite 700, Toronto, Ontario M4P 2Y3, Canada
(a division of Pearson Penguin Canada Inc.)
Penguin Books Ltd., 80 Strand, London WC2R 0RL, England
Penguin Group Ireland, 25 St. Stephen's Green, Dublin 2, Ireland (a division of Penguin Books Ltd.)
Penguin Group (Australia), 250 Camberwell Road, Camberwell, Victoria 3124, Australia
(a division of Pearson Australia Group Pty. Ltd.)
Penguin Books India Pvt. Ltd., 11 Community Centre, Panchsheel Park, New Delhi—110 017, India
Penguin Group (NZ), 67 Apollo Drive, Rosedale, North Shore 0745, Auckland, New Zealand (a division of Pearson New Zealand Ltd.)
Penguin Books (South Africa) (Pty.) Ltd., 24 Sturdee Avenue, Rosebank, Johannesburg 2196, South Africa

Penguin Books Ltd., Registered Offices: 80 Strand, London WC2R 0RL, England

While the author has made every effort to provide accurate telephone numbers and Internet addresses at the time of publication, neither the publisher nor the author assumes any responsibility for errors, or for changes that occur after publication. Further, the publisher does not have any control over and does not assume any responsibility for author or third-party websites or their content.

SOCK AND GLOVE

Copyright © 2005 by Miyako Kanamori
English translation by Wendy Matsamura
Photographs by Miyako Toyota
Photography in cooperation with Tinkerbell (Shibuya Jinnan shop)
Diagrams by Mitsuru Iijima
Book design by Kiyoko Wakayama Miki Wakayama L'espace

First American edition: June 2007
Originally published as *Tebukuro Inu to Kutsushita Zaru* in Japan by Bunka Shuppankyoku in 2005.

Home trade paperback ISBN: 978-1-55788-516-6

Printed in Mexico

10  9  8  7  6  5  4

Most Home books are available at special quantity discounts for bulk purchases for sales promotions, premiums, fund-raising, or educational use. Special books, or book excerpts, can also be created to fit specific needs. For details, write: Special Markets, Penguin Group (USA) Inc., 375 Hudson Street, New York, New York 10014.

# THINGS YOU SHOULD KNOW BEFORE GETTING STARTED

## 1 On selecting gloves and socks

You can find cotton work gloves at hardware and home-improvement stores. The heavy socks used to make the monkey can be found at home-improvement stores as well.

## 2 When sewing

Sewing can be done completely by hand. A backstitch is best for sewing everything but the facial features. Of course, it is acceptable to use a sewing machine as well. The seam allowance in this case should be approximately 0.2 inch.

The thread used is cotton sewing thread. Using a thin knitting wool or embroidery thread for sewing on the arms, tails, and so on to the body adds a nice touch. The same goes for sewing on buttons as the eyes or mouth.

## 3 The cotton stuffing

Local craft or fabric stores sell cotton stuffing for crafts. If your stuffing is made out of synthetic fiber, you can wash your dolls by putting them in netting and throwing them in the washing machine when they get dirty. Further, if you use a polypropylene-based cotton called "pellet" at the bottom of the dolls, they can sit up easily.

## 4 How to stuff the cotton

The cotton should be stuffed from the front end. Even if it looks slightly bumpy at first, this will become unnoticeable after the shape is adjusted later. The body type and facial expressions of the dolls will vary depending on how much cotton you use, so stuff according to your personal preference.

## 5 Putting on the buttons and stitching

It is difficult to sew on buttons or stitch something when it is filled with cotton. Scoop or pinch the cloth in your hands while sewing to make it easier.

As for the stitching knots, it is all right to leave these showing. If this bothers you, the following measures can be taken to hide the knot. At the beginning of stitching, stick the needle in a little bit away from where the stitching actually starts, push the needle back out where this should start, and pull hard so that the knot goes to the inside. At the end of the stitching after knotting, stick the needle back inside of the doll and push it back out a little bit away from the end of the actual stitch. Pull hard so that the knot goes to the inside and cut the excess thread.

## 6 Your one-of-a-kind doll

This book contains instructions for creating basic softy dolls, but the doll's whole expression changes depending on how much cotton is used, and whether you sew by hand or sewing machine. Further, the facial expressions differ according to the color, shape, and size of the buttons and beads used for the eyes and noses. Instead of trying to make exact replicas of the dolls pictured in this book, feel free to experiment. Have fun making one-of-a-kind dolls of your own!

I am Billy the dog.

I am Marcus the monkey.

We were once just some gloves and socks that

were going to be thrown away.

However, Mom turned us into a dog and

a monkey instead.

After that,

we visited many different places and played!

We wanted some new friends,

so one day, we placed a bunch of gloves

and socks on Mom's table.

We had many friends after that!

Rabbit page 48

Bear page 49

Dog page 50

Cat page 51

13

Sheep page 52

14

Girl page 53

We wanted even more,

so we placed a small mitten

and a sock on her feet.

Mouse page 54

Bird page 55

What do you get from a pink glove and a blue sock?

Pig page 56

22

Fish page 54

What about one black glove,

one white glove, and a long gray sock?

# Panda page 57

Elephant page 58

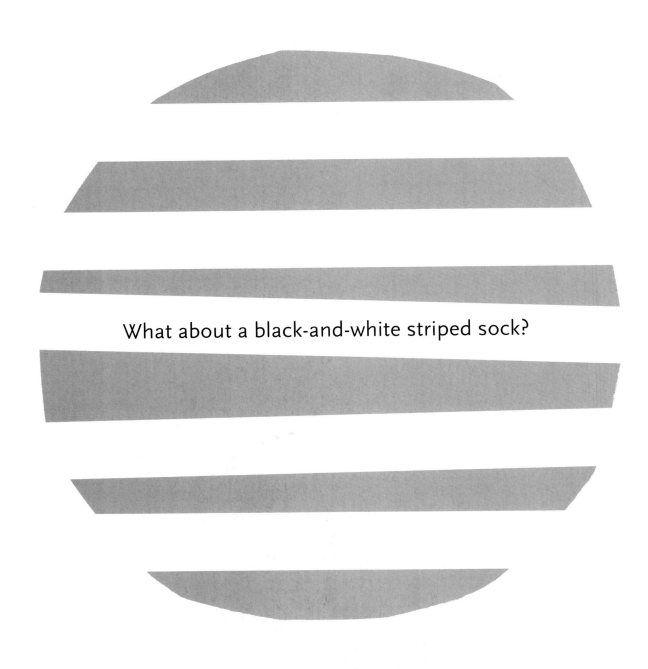

What about a black-and-white striped sock?

Zebra page 59

31

She even made us some clothes and hats.

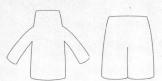

34

Dress • Hat page 61

We made so many friends.

. . . we are all very good friends!

And even though we fight sometimes . . .

Thanks, Mom!

So, how were we made in the first place?

## 1

Start with a pair of gloves.

## 2

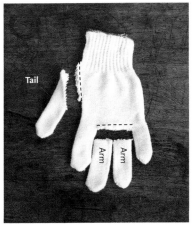

Flip one of the gloves inside out, and using scissors, cut away the thumb, middle, and ring finger. Following the dotted lines, sew the cutaway part closed, leaving approximately a 0.2-inch border from the cut area.

## 3

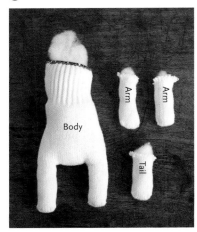

Flip all four parts right-side out and fill them all with cotton.

## 4

Fold the opening of the arms inside approximately 0.2 inch and sew each of them onto the body.

## 5

Fold the opening of the tail inside approximately 0.2 inch as well, and sew it onto the body.

## 6

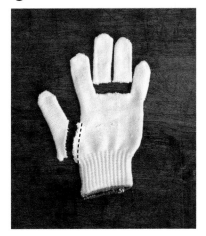

Take the other glove, flip it inside out, and cut away the thumb, middle, and ring fingers. Following the dotted line, sew the thumb part of the glove closed, leaving approximately a 0.2-inch border from the cut area.

## 7

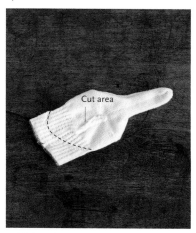

Fold the glove so that the cut area of the thumb becomes the center. Sew a curved line to close the glove (see dotted line).

## 8

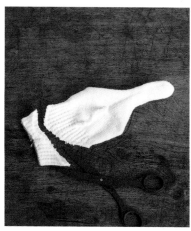

Cut along the curved line, leaving approximately a 0.2-inch border from the seam.

## 9

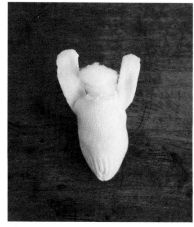

Flip the glove right-side out and fill it with cotton from the top of the head, excluding the ears.

## 10

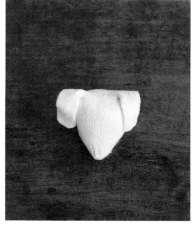

Sew the cotton-filled portion closed. Fold over the ears and pin them down lightly with thread.

## 11

Sew the head onto the body, using a pin while sewing to hold them together if necessary.

## 12

Use buttons for the eyes and nose, and use a backstitch to sew a circle around one eye. Create a belly button with thread.

Which face

do you like?

## 1

Start with a pair of socks.

## 2

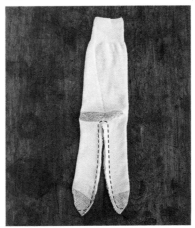

Flip one of the socks inside out, and fold it so that the heel is on top. Cut an opening from the toe to approximately 0.8 inch before the heel. Sew the cutaway part closed, leaving approximately 0.2 inch from the cut area.

## 3

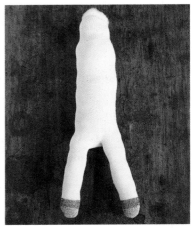

Flip the sock right-side out and fill with cotton. Since the top is where the head will be, make sure to fill it up so that it becomes round.

## 4

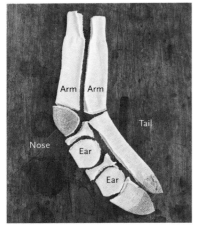

Flip the other sock inside out and cut as directed in the diagram.

## 5

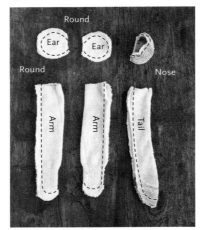

Sew each of the parts as directed by the red dotted lines. After sewing the end of the arms in a rounded shape, cut off the excess, leaving a 0.2-inch border from the seam. Gather and sew the nose part, shaping it so that it is round and three-dimensional.

## 6

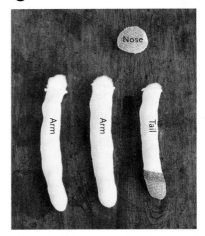

Flip each of the parts right-side out and fill the arms, tail, and nose with cotton.

## 7

Gather and sew the top of the head by pinching folds of the fabric together to create a rounded top, as shown in the diagram.

## 8

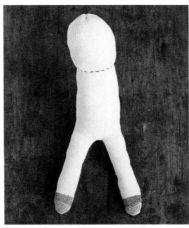

Stitch a line around the neck, then gather by pulling tightly, in order to make the neck thinner than the head.

## 9

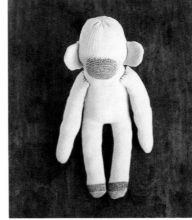

For the ears, nose, and arms, fold the openings inside approximately 0.2 inch and attach to the body.

## 10

Fold the opening of the tail inside approximately 0.2 inch as well and sew it onto the body.

## 11

Use buttons for the eyes and the nose.

## 12

Use a backstitch above the eyes and in the ears, and use thread to create a belly button and mouth.

# Rabbit page 10

1 Flip both gloves inside out and cut the fingers as shown in the diagram by the red solid lines. Sew as directed by the red dotted lines. Leave approximately a 0.2-inch border from the seam and cut the excess.

2 Flip the body, arms, and tail right-side out and fill with cotton. Fold the open parts of the arms and tail inside approximately 0.2 inch and sew them onto the body.

3 For the head, fold the glove so that the thumb area that was cut open (and sewn shut) is in the center (as shown in the diagram). Sew as directed by the red dotted lines and then cut away, leaving approximately a 0.2-inch border of space from the seam.

4 Flip the head right-side out and fill with cotton.

5 Fill the ears with cotton as well and sew the opening closed.

6 Sew the head onto the body. Use buttons for the eyes and the nose and a backstitch for the ears. Create a belly button with thread.

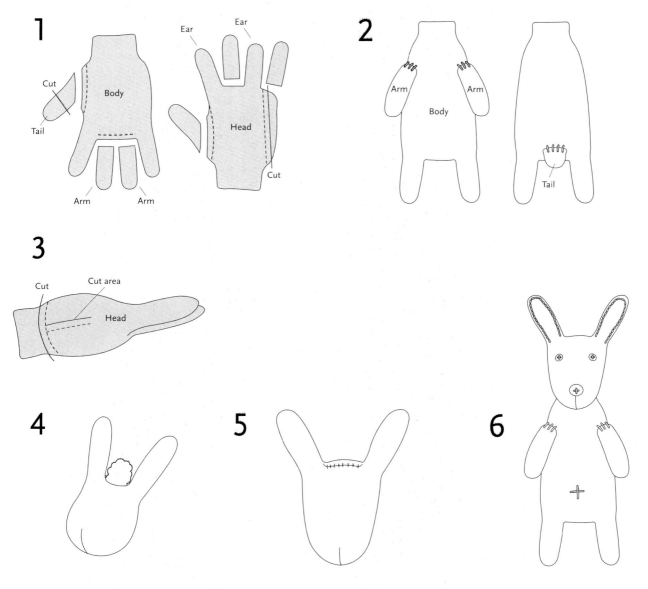

# Bear page 11

1 Flip both gloves inside out. Cut the fingers as directed by the diagram and the red solid lines. Sew along the red dotted lines.

2 Flip the body, arms, and tail right-side out. Stuff with cotton. Fold the openings of the arms and tail inside approximately 0.2 inch and sew them onto the body.

3 For the head, arrange the glove so that the thumb area that was cut open is on the bottom and sew along the red dotted line as directed in the diagram. Cut a border approximately 0.2 inch from the seam. Flip right-side out and fill with cotton.

4 Fold the back of the head like a caramel-candy wrapper (in order: left, right, bottom, then top) and sew shut. Flip the ears back right-side out, and sew them onto the head.

5 Sew the head onto the body, use buttons for the eyes and nose, and create a belly button with thread.

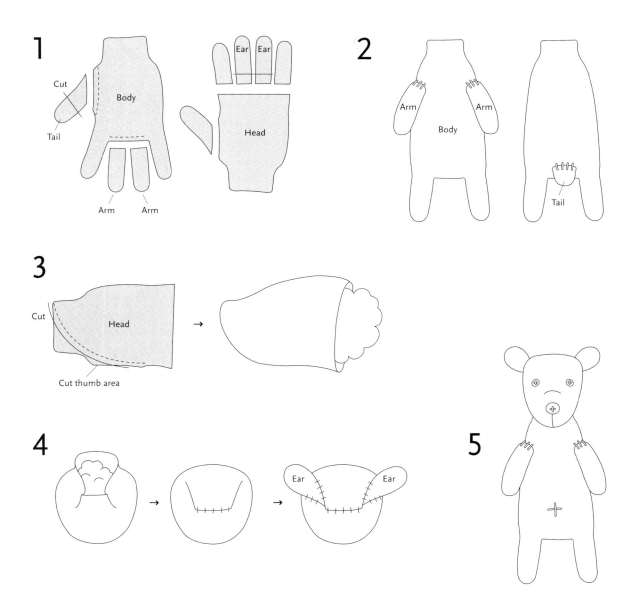

# Dog page 12

1 Flip each of the socks inside out and fold one of them so that the heel is on top. Cut as directed in the diagram by the red solid lines.

2 Sew the body, arms, ears, and tail as directed by the red dotted lines, then flip each of them right-side out. For the body, fold the elastic part of the sock inside. Fill each part, except for the ears, with cotton.

3 Flip the head right-side out and reinforce the side with the elastic with a pin. Fill it with cotton from the opening.

4 Fold the back of the head like a caramel-candy wrapper (in order: left, right, bottom, then top) and sew shut. Sew the opening of the ears onto the head as directed in the diagram.

5 Fold the bottom of the tip of the nose inside and then fold the upper part of the nose inside. Finally, fold both the left and right sides, leaving a little less than 0.4 inch on each side from the center of the nose. Sew shut.

6 Sew the head onto the body. Fold the opening of the arms and the tail approximately 0.2 inch inside and sew these onto the body as well.

7 Use buttons for the eyes and nose and thread for the belly button.

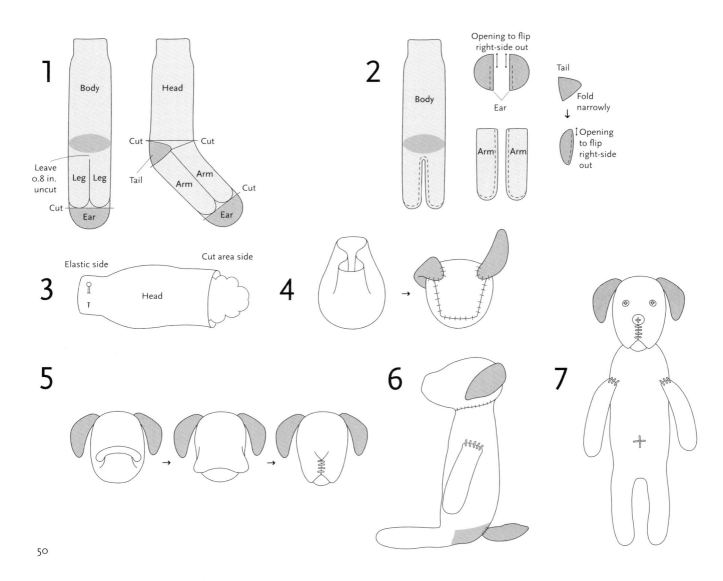

# Cat page 13

1 Flip both socks inside out. Take one sock and fold it so that the heel lies on top and cut as directed by the diagram and along the red solid lines.

2 Sew the body together as directed by the red dotted lines and leave an opening (the U-shaped downward-facing arrows) so that the sock can be flipped right-side out. Flip out and fill generously with cotton so that the head becomes round. After filling, sew the opening closed.

3 Sew together the red dotted line part of the ears, leaving an opening so it can be flipped right-side out. Flip out and sew together, folding the opening inside.

4 Sew the ears onto the head and tie knitting wool or ribbon around the neck.

5 Sew the red dotted line parts of the arms and tail, flip them right-side out, and fill with cotton. After folding the open parts inside approximately 0.2 inch, sew each onto the body.

6 Use buttons for the eyes and nose, and use thread for the whiskers and belly button.

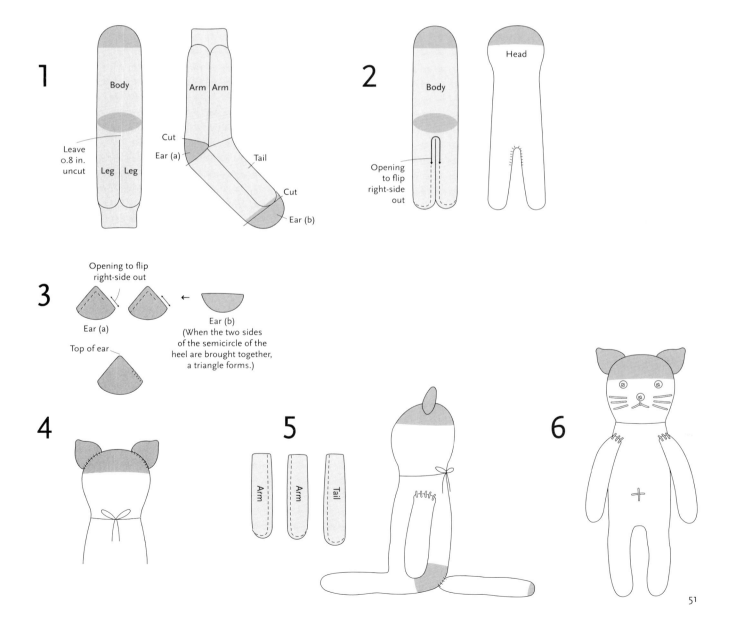

# Sheep page 14

1 Flip each of the socks inside out, and fold one of them so that the heel is on the top. Cut as directed in the diagram along the red solid lines.

2 Sew the body, arms, and tail as directed by the red dotted lines, then flip each of them right-side out. For the body, fold the elastic part of the sock inside. Fill each part with cotton.

3 Flip the head part right-side out and fill with cotton from the top opening. Carefully sew the bottom opening so that it has a diameter of approximately 1.6 inches.

4 Fold the back of the head like a caramel-candy wrapper (in order: left, right, bottom, then top) and sew shut.

5 For the ears, sew along the red dotted lines and then flip right-side out. Fold the opening back inside, and sew them onto the body.

6 Sew the head onto the body. Fold the openings of the arms and tail inside approximately 0.2 inch and sew each part onto the body. Create eyes, a nose, and a belly button using thread.

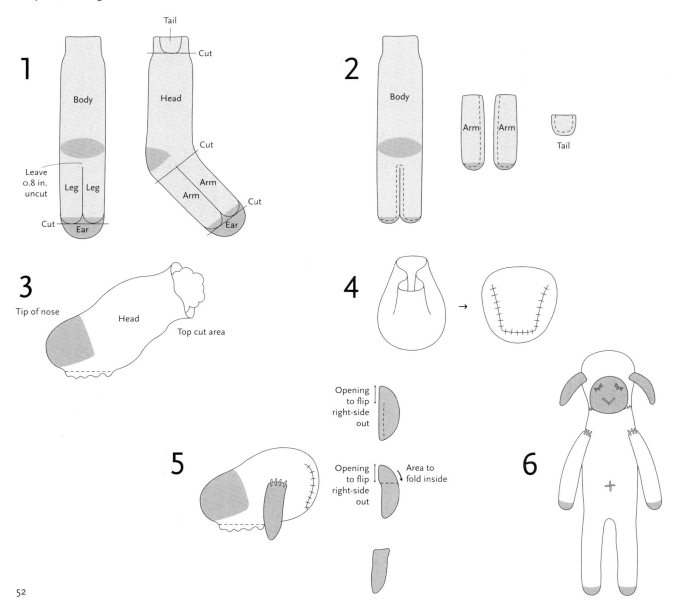

# Girl page 15

1 Flip each of the socks inside out and fold one of them so that the heel is on top. Cut as directed in the diagram along the red solid lines.

2 Sew the body and arms as shown by the red dotted lines, then flip each of them right-side out.

3 Fold over the ears as directed in the diagram and sew along the red dotted line.

4 For the braids, cut an opening into the center and divide into two. Twist and reinforce with thread. Repeat on the other side.

5 For the head, flip back right-side out and then fill with cotton. Gather and sew the opening so that it has a diameter of 2 inches. Sew the ears onto the head and sew the braids slightly above the ears.

6 Sew the head onto the body and sew the arms on after folding the openings inside approximately 0.2 inch. Use buttons for the eyes, and create eyelashes, a nose, a mouth, and a belly button with thread.

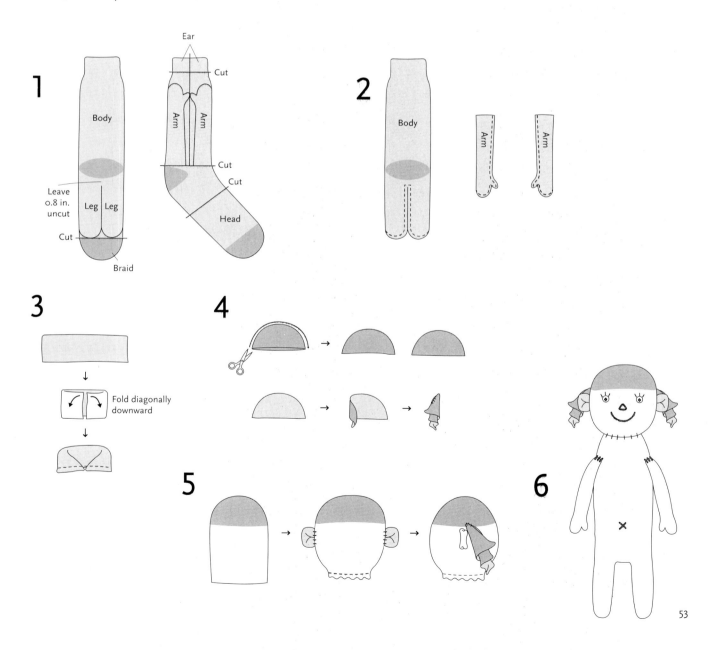

## Mouse page 18

1 Cut the mittens as directed in the diagram along the red solid lines.

2 Fill the body with cotton and sew the opening shut. Cut the ears, making sure that the lengths are even.

3 Sew the ears and tail onto the body. Make a knot at the end of the tail so that it does not unravel. Use buttons for the eyes and a round wooden bead for the nose.

**Bonus:** A fish can be made using the unused side of the mitten.

Sew the thumb opening shut and fill with cotton. Decide where the tail is going to be, gather and sew. Use a button for the eye.

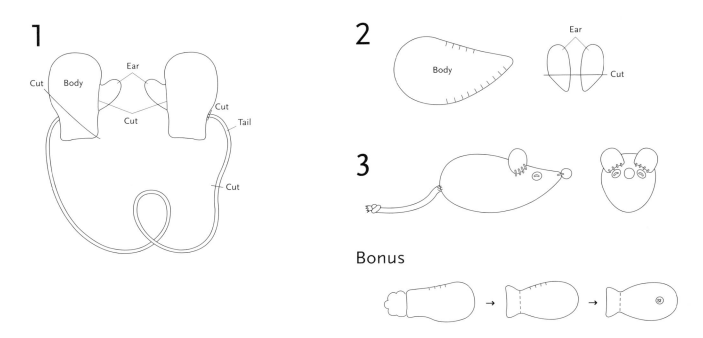

**Bonus**

## Fish page 23

1 Cut one sock as directed in the diagram.

2 Fill the body with cotton and create a tail by inserting part of the sock into the opening of the body.

3 Slightly fold the opening of the body inside, then gather and sew together with the tail. Use a button for the eye.

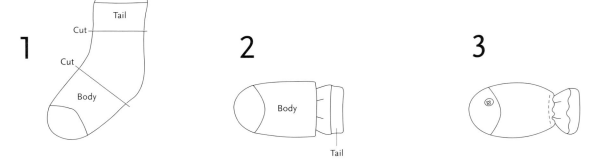

# Bird page 19

1 Cut the socks as directed in the diagram.

2 Turn the body sideways. After deciding on the length of the tail, slightly gather, sew, and fill the body with cotton. Gather and sew the opening shut.

3 Fill the head with cotton, and gather and sew the opening shut, leaving a small amount of give so that you can push the button that will become the beak partially inside. Sew the button securely in place. (You can use a wood or plastic toggle button, the kind that is used for coats, etc.)

4 Sew the head onto the body.

5 Use a blanket stitch to sew the opening of the wing shut.

6 Sew the front part of the wings onto the body and use buttons for the eyes.

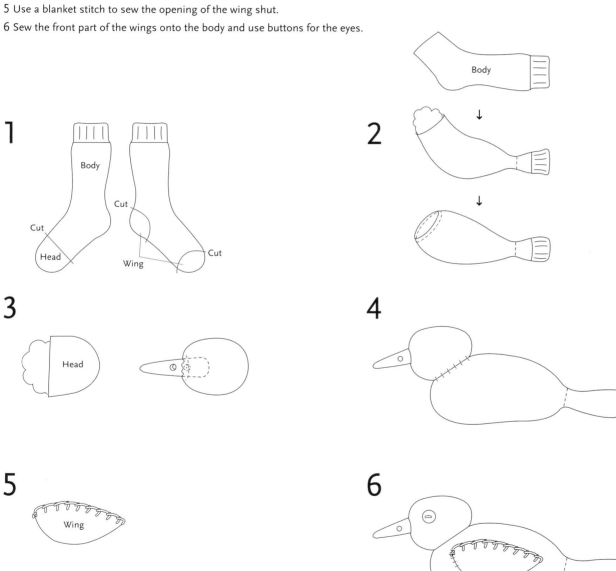

# Pig page 22

1 Flip both of the gloves inside out, cut off the fingers as directed in the diagram, and sew the cut area of the body and the tail shut. In many wool gloves, the thumb is attached to the surface of the palm of the hand. In such cases, sew the cut area of the thumb shut. The same applies to the cut area of the head.

2 Flip the body and arms right-side out and fold the openings of the arms inside approximately 0.2 inch. Sew each onto the body. For the tail, after flipping it back right-side out, twist and reinforce with thread.

3 For the head, make sure that the back of the hand part of the glove is at the top center, then sew as directed by the red dotted lines and cut a 0.2-inch border from the seam. Flip it back right-side out and fill with cotton.

4 Fold the back of the head like a caramel-candy wrapper (in order: left, right, bottom, then top) and sew shut. Flip the ears back right-side out, push them into the head, and sew as directed in the diagram.

5 Sew the head onto the body. Use round wooden beads for the eyes and a large button for the nose.

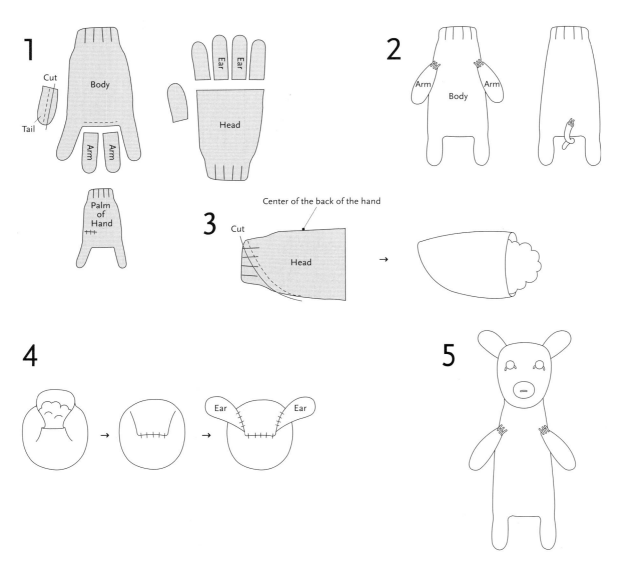

# Panda page 26

1 Flip the pair of white gloves inside out, cut as directed in the diagram, and sew as directed by the red dotted line. Do not flip the black gloves inside out; just cut as directed in the diagram.

2 Flip the tail right-side out and fill with cotton. Fill the arms and legs with cotton. For the ears that are double-layered, sew along the red dotted lines and flip right-side out. Do not fill with cotton.

3 Place the legs inside the bottom cut area of the body and sew along the red dotted line. Flip back right-side out and fill the body with cotton. Fold the opening of the arms inside approximately 0.2 inch, and sew them onto the body.

4 For the head, make sure that the thumb cut area is on the bottom and sew along the red dotted line. Cut along the seam, leaving approximately a 0.2-inch border from the seam. Flip the head right-side out and fill with cotton.

5 Fold the back of the head like a caramel-candy wrapper (in order: left, right, bottom, then top) and sew shut. Flip the ears right-side out and sew them onto the head as directed in the diagram.

6 Sew the head onto the body, sew the eyes on, and use a button for the nose.

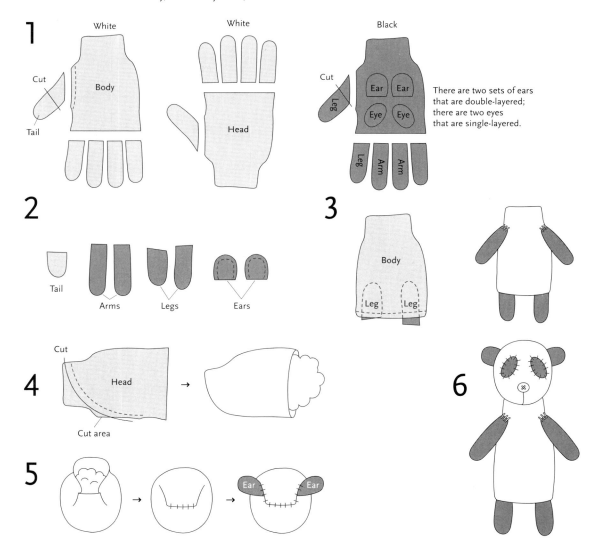

# Elephant page 27

1 Flip each of the socks inside out and cut as directed in the diagram.

2 For the arms and the legs, make sure the inside of the sock is facing out and the elastic part is on top. Shape each part into a cylinder. Sew the circles that were cut for the bottom of the arms and legs onto the bottom of the cylinders (the inside of the socks should be facing outward). Flip right-side out and fill with cotton. Use a blanket stitch for a nice accent. Make four identical parts.

3 Place the legs inside the bottom cut area of the body and sew along the red dotted line. Flip back right-side out (the legs will now pop out) and fill with cotton. Fold the opening of the arms inside approximately 0.2 inch and sew onto the body. Slightly gather and sew the opening of the neck area.

4 For the head, fold the tip of the nose back approximately 0.2 inch and sew. Also sew as directed by the red dotted line. Flip the head right-side out and fill with cotton. Fold the back of the head like a caramel-candy wrapper (in order: left, right, bottom, then top) and sew shut.

5 Flip the ears back right-side out. Pinch the center of the cut area and pin down as directed in the diagram. Fold the cut area approximately 0.2 inch inside and sew onto the head. Remove the pins.

6 Flip the tail back right-side out, sew the cut area with a blanket stitch, and sew onto the buttocks. Sew the head onto the body and create eyes using thread.

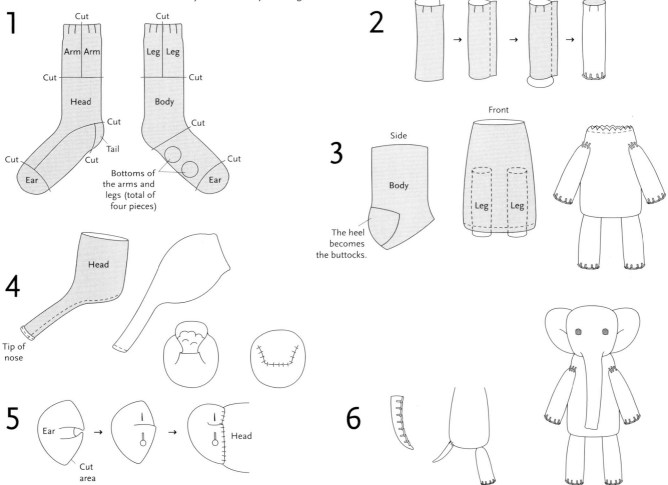

# Zebra page 30

1 Flip one of the socks inside out; keep one right-side out. Cut both as directed in the diagram.

2 Fill the body with cotton, fold both sides like a caramel-candy wrapper (in order, left, right, bottom, then top), and sew shut.

3 Fill the head with cotton and fold the opening like a caramel-candy wrapper. Sew shut.

4 For the ears, place one on top of the other with the sock facing inward and sew along the red dotted line. Flip back right-side out.

5 Wrap a narrow woolen thread or an embroidery thread ten times around a piece of cardboard that is 2 inches square. Remove the cardboard and tie the thread at the bottom. Cut evenly across, approximately 0.2 inch from the top to create a tassel. Make eight of these tassels.

6 Sew seven of the tassels from the top to the bottom of the zebra's head. Sew the ears on after folding the opening inside approximately 0.2 inch.

7 For the tail, create a cylinder shape with the outer surface of the sock facing outward. Sew as directed by the red dotted line. Flip back right-side out and place the remaining tassel inside. Sew onto the tail.

8 Sew the four legs into cylinders as well. Flip back right-side out and fill with cotton.

9 For the four legs and the tail, fold the openings inside approximately 0.2 inch and then sew onto the body. Sew the head on and use buttons for the eyes.

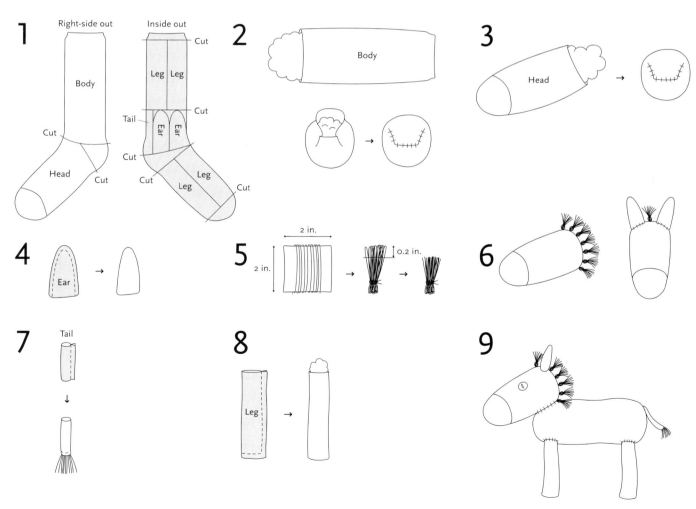

## Shirt page 34

1 Flip one of the socks inside out (use either men's or women's knee socks) and cut as directed in the diagram.

2 Fold back approximately 0.3 inch of the sleeve, sew with the outside surface facing inward, and flip back right-side out.

3 Depending on the width of the sleeve, adjust the position onto which it is attached to the body, cut an oval opening in the body, and insert the sleeve inside of the hole. Sew as directed by the red dotted line. Fold the hem over approximately 0.3 inch and sew. Repeat with the other sleeve.

4 Flip back right-side out.

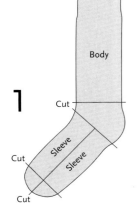

**1**

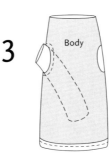

**2** →

**3**

**4**

## Pants page 34

1 Cut the fabric as directed in the diagram by the red solid lines.

2 On the back, there are two cuts for the tail opening on the pants. Fold each flap of the tail opening inside. Sew a square around it.

3 Create a 0.4-inch hem in the front and the back and then sew. Bring the front and the back together with what will be the outside facing inward. Sew as directed by the red dotted line. Make a 0.8-inch fold in the waist area and sew. Create two holes for a drawstring.

4 Flip back right-side out and insert a drawstring.

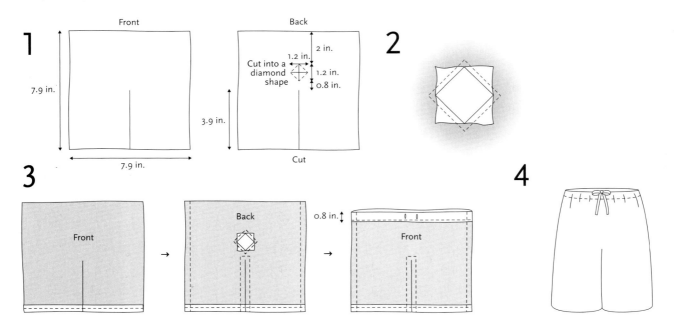

# Dress page 35

1 Cut the fabric as directed in the diagram. We used a kitchen towel for the fabric so we did not have to hem it. If hemming is necessary, fold in approximately 0.3 inch and then sew.
2 Fold the curved neck and sleeves inside approximately 0.3 inch and then sew.
3 Place the two pieces together with what will be the outside facing inward. Leave a 0.3-inch seam allowance and sew the shoulders and both underarms together.
4 Flip right-side out.

**1**
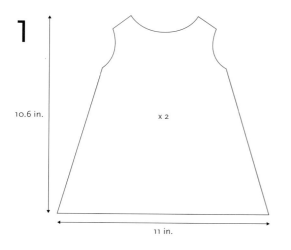
10.6 in.

x 2

11 in.

**2**
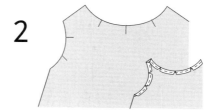

**3** 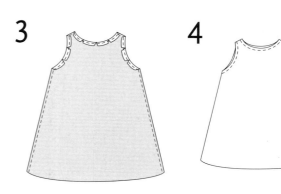 **4**

# Hat page 35

1 Cut the fabric as directed in the diagram. We used burlap as the fabric. You can also use coarse linen cloth, sold in fabric stores.
2 Create a rounded brim by following the diagram. Sew it onto the top.
3 Tie a ribbon around the hat.

**1**
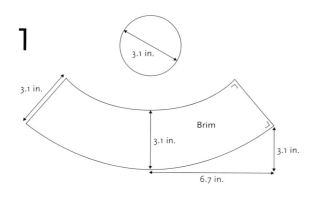
3.1 in.

3.1 in.

Brim

3.1 in.

3.1 in.

6.7 in.

**2**  **3**

# INDEX

## Items made from gloves

## Items made from socks